Roge

By U

https://campsite.bio/unitedlibrary

Table of Contents

Disclaimer

This biography book is a work of nonfiction based on the public life of a famous person. The author has used publicly available information to create this work. While the author has thoroughly researched the subject and attempted to depict it accurately, it is not meant to be an exhaustive study of the subject. The views expressed in this book are those of the author alone and do not necessarily reflect those of any organization associated with the subject. This book should not be taken as an endorsement, legal advice, or any other form of professional advice. This book was written for entertainment purposes only.

Introduction

Dive into the riveting story of Roger Federer, the Swiss maestro who graced the tennis world with his elegance, skill, and unmatched sportsmanship. Born on August 8, 1981, Federer's remarkable career unfolded as he ascended to the pinnacle of men's singles tennis, holding the world No. 1 ranking for an astounding 310 weeks, including an unprecedented 237 consecutive weeks. This tennis virtuoso finished as the year-end No. 1 five times, leaving an indelible mark on the sport.

Federer's journey to tennis greatness began with his Wimbledon junior championship in 1998, and in 2003, at the age of 21, he secured his first major singles title at Wimbledon. The following years witnessed a golden era for Federer, with 20 major men's singles titles, a record eight Wimbledon titles, and five US Open titles, establishing him as one of the greatest players in the history of the game.

This compelling biography explores Federer's impact beyond individual accomplishments, from leading the Switzerland Davis Cup team to victory in 2014 to securing an Olympic doubles gold in 2008 with Stan Wawrinka. A versatile all-court player, Federer's grace and transformation from a fiery junior to a widely admired sportsman are thoroughly examined. His philanthropic endeavors, including the establishment of the Roger Federer Foundation aimed at aiding impoverished children in southern Africa, showcase a champion both on and off the court.

Discover the life and legacy of Roger Federer, a tennis icon whose finesse and contribution to the sport extend far beyond the baseline.

Roger Federer

Roger Federer (born August 8, 1981 in Basel; domiciled in Berneck) is a former Swiss tennis player.

He spent a total of 310 weeks at the top of the world rankings, including a record 237 weeks in a row. He was also the oldest player to top the rankings to date. Federer also finished the years 2004 to 2007 and 2009 at the top of the world rankings. In the statistics of Grand Slam titles won in the men's singles, he is in third place with 20 titles won, behind Novak Đoković (24) and Rafael Nadal (22). Federer won 103 singles and eight doubles titles in his 25-year career.

Federer is the first player to win three Grand Slam titles in one season (2004, 2006 and 2007). He is one of eight players to have won all four Grand Slam tournaments at least once during their career. With eight singles titles, he is the record winner of the Wimbledon Championships. He has won the Australian Open six times, the US Open five times and the French Open once. With six victories, he is the joint record holder with Đoković at the ATP Finals, has won 28 Masters tournaments and is the record winner of the ATP Tour 500 series with 24 titles.

Federer has been voted World Sportsman of the Year five times (from 2005 to 2008 and 2018), more often than any other athlete.

Personal

Roger Federer, the son of a Swiss father (Robert Federer) and a South African mother (Lynette), grew up in the Basel suburbs of Riehen and Wasserhaus in Münchenstein together with his sister Diana, who is two years older. According to Federer, the English pronunciation of his first name, which does not correspond to the French pronunciation [rɔˈʒeː] that is otherwise common in Switzerland, is also related to his mother's origins. Federer speaks fluent English and French as well as German and can therefore easily switch between these languages in press conferences or interviews. In addition to his Swiss passport, he also holds a South African passport.

His wife Mirka Federer-Vavrinec, a former Swiss tennis player, had to end her career in 2002 due to a foot injury. The two met on the sidelines of the 2000 Olympic Games in Sydney. On April 11, 2009, they married in Riehen near Basel with close family and friends, and on July 23, 2009, they became parents to twin daughters. Their twin sons were born on May 6, 2014. Vavrinec is said to have had a considerable mental influence on Federer.

Roger Federer had himself declared unfit for military service on medical grounds because he had back problems. This led to discussions among the Swiss public, as more and more men of the same age group have been declared unfit for military service for years. (In 2006, just 65% of men in Switzerland were still fit for military service).

In December 2003, the tennis pro set up the *Roger Federer Foundation,* which provides financial support for aid projects for children, mainly in southern Africa and Switzerland. The purpose of the foundation is to promote educational projects and youth sport, particularly for children from financially disadvantaged backgrounds. Since its establishment, around 68 million Swiss francs have been invested, reaching over 2 million children.

Federer was also involved in tsunami relief projects after the 2004 Indian Ocean earthquake and played several charity tournaments to support those affected. In April 2006, Roger Federer was the first Swiss to be appointed an international UNICEF ambassador. Because of this voluntary commitment, he was presented with the Child Award by the *Kinderlachen* association in 2006.

Federer has lived in Valbella since 2015, where he moved from Bäch. He also has another residence in Dubai.

Tennis career

Childhood and youth (1984-1998)

Unlike other greats in tennis history, Roger Federer did not make international headlines at a young age. His parents were not the typical tennis parents, he chose this path himself. As in his later professional career, he was characterized by continuous development. Spectacular successes only came in his late teens. There were no large-scale reports as there were with tennis talents such as Andre Agassi, Martina Hingis or Steffi Graf. The Swiss started playing tennis at the age of three and joined the TC Old Boys tennis club at the age of eight. There, his development was significantly advanced by coaches Adolf Kacovský and Peter Carter.

After his first national successes, Federer decided at the age of twelve to concentrate entirely on tennis and not to further develop his equally strong talent in football - he was a junior at FC Concordia Basel. In 1995, he moved to the Swiss national training center in Ecublens. From then on, the Swiss association supported Federer, who won seven Swiss junior championship titles between 1995 and 1997. In 1995, he only reached the round of 16 at the Orange Bowl in Miami, the last major international junior tournament of the year. Nevertheless, he regarded his performance as his greatest international success to date. From 1997, Federer increasingly took part in international tournaments and won his first major international junior title in Prato in May.

It was also during this time that he decided to leave school at the age of 16 in favor of a career in tennis. Federer took the risk and his breakthrough on the junior tour came as early as 1998; in January he reached the semi-finals of the Australian Open and went on to win the singles and doubles titles at Wimbledon. These successes enabled him to take part in his first tournaments on the professional tour. He made his debut on the ATP Tour in Gstaad in July 1998 and reached his first professional quarter-final in Toulouse in September. By winning the Orange Bowl in December, his last junior tournament, Federer secured first place in the junior rankings at the end of the year. This was not only a great prestigious success for him, but also the springboard for his final entry into the professional tour.

Start of professional career (1999-2000)

His reputation as junior world champion helped the now 17-year-old to gain a foothold on the professional tour. Over the course of his first professional season, he received a total of eight wildcards for tournaments on the ATP Tour. This enabled him to surpass his goal of being ranked among the 200 best players in the world at the end of the season as early as the spring. On his Davis Cup debut, Federer won the singles, helping his country to reach the quarter-finals of the competition. In the summer, he made his professional debut at Roland Garros and Wimbledon, where he was eliminated in the first round. Later in the year, he showed his strength in indoor tournaments. He reached his first semi-final on the ATP Tour in Vienna, making it into the top 100 players in the world rankings; he finished the season ranked 64th.

For the 2000 season, Federer set himself the goal of establishing himself among the top 50 players in the world. He continued to prove himself as an indoor specialist, even though he achieved success in outdoor tournaments for the first time. He reached his first final on the professional tour in Marseille at the beginning of the year, which he lost to his older compatriot Marc Rosset. Having already made the leap into the world's top 50, the season's target was revised upwards to 25th place. In April, Federer announced his separation from the Swiss Association and thus also from his coach Peter Carter. He justified the move by saying that he was now in a position to stand on his own two feet and had therefore decided to take this path. He hired the Swede Peter Lundgren as his new coach, who recognized his talent but still saw potential for development in his 18-year-old protégé.

Federer suffered several first-round defeats in the
summer and his record at important tournaments
remained modest. Nevertheless, his federation
nominated him for the Olympic Games in Sydney, where
he reached the semi-finals. However, he was defeated in
both matches for a medal. He reached his second final on
the ATP Tour at his home tournament in Basel. There he
was defeated by the Swede Thomas Enqvist. Finishing
29th at the end of the year, he narrowly missed his
season target. In the winter, he hired Pierre Paganini as
his fitness coach in order to meet the physical demands of
the world's top players.

From first title to Wimbledon success (2001-2003)

Federer started the 2001 season with the aim of winning
his first tournament in his third professional season and
being ranked among the top 15 players in the world. After
winning the 2001 Hopman Cup with Martina Hingis in
January, he achieved his first goal in February. At his third
attempt, Federer won a tournament final for the first time
in Milan against Julien Boutter. In the Davis Cup, he
played a decisive role in Switzerland's first-round victory
over the USA with two singles wins. In the quarter-finals
of the competition against France, he declared that he
would no longer take part in the Davis Cup under Davis
Cup coach Jakob Hlasek. A few weeks later, Federer's
contract with Hlasek was terminated, reflecting Federer's

increased importance in Swiss tennis. In the following clay court season, he reached his first quarter-final at a Grand Slam tournament. He started Wimbledon as number 15 in the world. There he met seven-time champion Pete Sampras in the round of 16. After five sets, the 19-year-old Swiss was the winner, ending Sampras' streak of 31 consecutive victories at Wimbledon. However, he lost the following quarter-final match against Tim Henman from Great Britain. Federer suffered a groin injury during the tournament, forcing him to take a seven-week break. He was not fit again until the US Open in late summer, but lost to Andre Agassi in the round of 16. A place in the final in Basel during the following indoor season was not enough to realize the possible entry into the Tennis Masters Cup of the best eight players of the season based on the results of the first half of the season. Federer ended the season in 13th place in the world rankings.

At the beginning of the 2002 season, he won his second career title in Sydney. At the Australian Open, however, he lost in the round of 16, as he did in the final in Milan. In March, he reached his first final at a Masters Series tournament in Miami, but lost the match against Andre Agassi in four sets. A few weeks later, he reached his second final at a tournament of this category in Hamburg. This time, Federer won the final against the Russian Marat Safin. The 20-year-old Federer traveled to Paris as the second-placed player in the Champions Race. Here he surprisingly lost in the first round to Hicham Arazi. He was also eliminated in the opening round at Wimbledon. The Swiss player, who was rated as the fifth-best player at the tournament by the bookmakers, lost in three sets to Croatian Mario Ančić.

Meanwhile, there was open talk of a Grand Slam blockade for Federer. The Swiss (who was already being touted as a future multiple Grand Slam winner) rarely seemed to be able to play his best tennis at the four tournaments of the highest category. Up until the US Open, Federer had only won one match in four tournaments. His game suffered from thoughts of the accidental death of his former coach Peter Carter in South Africa at the beginning of August 2002. In New York, Federer was again eliminated in the round of 16. Nevertheless, he managed to qualify for the Tennis Masters Cup, as he always reached at least the quarter-finals in five tournaments during the indoor season and won his fourth tournament in Vienna. He was the only player apart from Carlos Moyá to qualify for the tournament without reaching a Grand Slam quarter-final in the course of the season. Federer won his three group matches to reach the semi-finals against world number one Lleyton Hewitt. In a close match, he squandered several opportunities and ultimately lost 5:7 in the third set. He ended the season in 6th place in the world rankings.

Coach Lundgren's goal for the 2003 season was to break into the top four of the world rankings. In addition, Federer continued to set himself the goal of winning a Grand Slam tournament. At his first chance to do so, he lost to David Nalbandian in the round of 16 of the Australian Open; after five sets he was defeated by the Argentinian. Over the next few months, he reached four finals on the tour and won his first titles of the season in Marseille, Dubai and Munich. In Rome, he was also unable to take advantage of the opportunity to win a second Masters Series title. In the Davis Cup, Federer won five of his first six matches and reached the semi-finals of this competition with Switzerland for the first time in his career. As in the previous year, the world number five was one of the tournament favorites ahead of the French Open. However, after yet another first-round defeat (against Luis Horna) at a Grand Slam tournament, he faced ridicule from the press. The reason for Federer's lack of success at major tournaments was attributed to a mental weakness.

After the French Open, the Swiss began his preparations for the tournament in Wimbledon at the Gerry Weber Open in Halle. He won his fourth title of the season there, setting a new personal best for the season. At Wimbledon, he was seeded third by the bookmakers this year and reached the quarter-final stage of a Grand Slam tournament for the first time in eight appearances. After recovering from a back injury at the beginning of the second week of the tournament due to lengthy rain interruptions, he met Andy Roddick in the semi-finals. Federer won 61 shots in three sets with only twelve unforced errors, taking him into the first Grand Slam final of his career. Although the Australian Mark Philippoussis forced him into a tie-break twice in the final, he was still defeated in the end and Federer won his first Grand Slam title. He had thus achieved his goal for the season and the mocking voices fell silent.

After winning Wimbledon, Federer also entered the battle for first place in the world rankings. Over the next few weeks, he missed several opportunities to reach this position. For example, he lost to Roddick in the semi-finals in Canada after leading 4:2 in the deciding set. In Cincinnati and at the US Open, however, he lost to David Nalbandian. In the Davis Cup semi-final against Australia, Federer also had to concede the match against Lleyton Hewitt after leading 2:0 in the third set at 5:3. Despite his sixth win of the season during the indoor season in Vienna, the top of the world rankings was no longer within Federer's reach this season. However, he ended his season with a success at the Masters Cup in Houston. As in the previous year, he won his three group matches and beat Roddick, who was already the world number one, in the semi-finals. In the final, he defeated Andre Agassi in three sets to win his first world title. Federer ended the

2003 season at No. 2 in the world rankings. The separation from coach Lundgren in December 2003, which Federer justified with signs of wear and tear and the feeling that he needed something new, caused some astonishment.

In first place in the world rankings (2004-2008)

Federer was criticized in public for parting ways with his successful coach. But despite doubts about his form and not rushing to find a new coach, he played his way through to the round of 16 at the 2004 Australian Open without dropping a set. He beat Hewitt and Nalbandian in four sets each, two players who both had positive records against him. After beating the world number two Juan Carlos Ferrero, he reached the tournament final. He beat his opponent Marat Safin in three sets in the final to win the second Grand Slam title of his career. At the same time, he also conquered the top spot in the world rankings and remained there until August 17, 2008, winning three more titles before the French Open in May, including the Masters Series tournaments in Indian Wells and Hamburg. In Paris, however, he was defeated in the third round by three-time title winner Gustavo Kuerten. Federer then won another double on the grass courts of Halle and Wimbledon. In the Wimbledon final, Andy Roddick took a set off him, unlike in the semi-final the previous year, but Federer ultimately defended his title. In Gstaad and Toronto, he extended his winning streak to 23 matches until he lost his opening match in Cincinnati.

A bigger disappointment for Federer, however, was his second-round defeat at the Olympic Games in Athens against Tomáš Berdych from the Czech Republic. The Swiss not only came to Athens as a clear medal candidate, but also as his country's flag bearer at the opening ceremony. On the other hand, this defeat was also the starting point for another winning streak. At the US Open in New York, he was only forced over the full five-set distance by Andre Agassi in the quarter-finals. In the final, he conceded just six games in three sets to Lleyton Hewitt on the way to his third Grand Slam title of the season. He was the first player since the Swede Mats Wilander in 1988 to achieve this success. Federer had to cancel the subsequent indoor season almost completely due to a torn muscle fiber. However, he was fit again in time for the Masters Cup. There he reached the final unbeaten and met Hewitt again. He defeated the former world number one for the sixth time this season and thus further extended his position at the top of the world rankings. In the 2004 season, he did not lose any of his eleven finals and won all 18 matches against opponents from the top 10.

Federer signed Australian Tony Roche as his new coach for the new 2005 season. Roche, who had already led players to several Grand Slam successes as coach to Ivan Lendl and Patrick Rafter, was to assist Federer in particular at the important tournaments. The special focus for this season was on the French Open, which Federer had not yet won in his career to date. The winning streak that Federer brought with him from the previous season was broken in the semi-final at the Australian Open against Marat Safin after more than four hours of play. This was followed by four tournament victories in a row, including the Swiss winning the double at the Masters tournaments in Indian Wells and Miami for the first time. He turned around a 0:2 set deficit against Rafael Nadal in the Miami final. The latter took second place in the world rankings thanks to regular successes on clay courts and increasingly closed the gap on Federer. After Federer's sixth title of the season in Hamburg, he met Nadal again in the semi-finals in Paris. This time, the Swiss lost in four sets. Although Federer had achieved his best result to date at the French Open, he remained without a Grand Slam title as the season progressed.

However, the defeat in France was the start of the longest winning streak of his career at the time. At Wimbledon, he only dropped one set on his way to the title hat-trick, and at the US Open he beat Andre Agassi in four sets in his last Grand Slam final. He brought a winning streak of

31 matches in a row to the Masters Cup at the end of the year, which he extended to 35 by reaching the tournament final. Here he faced David Nalbandian, against whom he had won the last four encounters, after the first five matches had all gone to the Argentinian. After two tie-breaks, the world number one was leading 2:0 in the sets. But the longer the match went on, the more Federer physically deteriorated. Although he was able to turn a 0:4 deficit into a 6:5 lead in the final set, Federer ended the match as the loser. This not only broke the fifth-longest winning streak in professional tennis, but also his record of 24 consecutive final match victories. In addition, with 81 wins and 4 defeats, the Swiss missed the chance to equal John McEnroe's statistically best professional season from 1984 (82 wins with 3 defeats). Nevertheless, Federer ended the season at No. 1 in the world rankings after missing the chance to win his third Masters Cup title in a row.

He began the 2006 season with two tournament victories, including his seventh Grand Slam title at the Australian Open. In Dubai, however, he lost again to Nadal in the final, ending the record streak of 56 consecutive victories on hard courts that began in Rotterdam the previous year. This was the starting signal for the numerous duels they were to have in the coming weeks and months. Before the clay court season began, Federer won the Indian Wells and Miami tournaments again. On clay, he reached the final at the Masters tournaments in Monte Carlo and Rome. He was defeated by Nadal in both matches, although he had match points in Rome. The final between Federer and Nadal also took place in Paris. After winning the first set, Federer missed further chances and lost to Nadal for the fifth time in a row, his first defeat in his eighth Grand Slam final. Nevertheless, he had established himself as the second-best clay court player in the world over the course of the season.

At Wimbledon, he played his way to the final without dropping a set on his way to his fourth title in a row. There he once again faced the world number two Nadal. The Spaniard was able to take a set off Federer, but in the end the Swiss celebrated his eighth Grand Slam title in total. He began another winning streak at the US Open. For the third time, he defeated Andy Roddick in a Grand Slam final and for the second time since 2004, he won three Grand Slam titles in one season. For the first time in three years, Federer also took part in the indoor season without injury. With his tournament victory in Madrid, he broke the record held by Jimmy Connors, who had topped the world rankings for 160 weeks without interruption in the 1970s.

Following the tournament in Madrid, Federer also won his home tournament in Basel for the first time after several unsuccessful attempts, beating Chile's Fernando González in the final. He then traveled to the Masters Cup in Shanghai. There he again reached the final without defeat in the group stage, losing just seven games in three sets against the American James Blake on his way to his third title at the year-end tournament. Federer thus ended his third consecutive season at the top of the world rankings, a feat previously only achieved by Jimmy Connors, John McEnroe, Ivan Lendl and Pete Sampras. The 2006 season was the best season of Federer's career and one of the most successful in history. He won twelve tournaments and reached the final 16 times in 17 tournaments played, which is still unsurpassed today.

In the 2006 season, Federer only needed to win the French Open to achieve the greatest success in tennis, the Grand Slam. Apart from the American Don Budge (1938), only the Australian Rod Laver (1962 and 1969) has ever achieved this. Laver himself declared in January 2006 that he believed Federer could win the Grand Slam. Federer took the first step in this direction at the Australian Open, where he became the first player since Björn Borg in 1980 to win a Grand Slam tournament without dropping a set. In the course of the clay court season that followed, the Swiss separated from his coach Tony Roche, defeated his rival Nadal for the first time on clay in Hamburg and ended Nadal's streak of 81 victories on this surface. However, the hunt for a Grand Slam win ended again at the French Open, where Federer reached the final again but was unable to repeat his Hamburg success against Nadal.

At the start of the season, Federer defended his title at the Australian Open and won the tournament for the third time. In Indian Wells, he lost to Guillermo Cañas in the opening match, ending his run of seven tournament wins and 41 victories in a row. As in the previous year, the Wimbledon final was also a duel between Federer and Nadal. In his fifth final there, the Swiss was forced to go the full distance of five sets for the first time, but after the match he collected his fifth consecutive winner's trophy. In doing so, he equaled the Open Era record of Sweden's Björn Borg. In Cincinnati, he won the 50th title of his career against James Blake. Federer also won the US Open once again, prevailing in three sets against Novak Đoković. This was the fourth year in a row since 2004 that he had won both Wimbledon and the US Open. Once again, Federer had only suffered a Grand Slam defeat in the final of the French Open. Federer proved to be beatable at other tournaments, however. For the first time since 2003, he triumphed at fewer than three Masters Series tournaments. Only in Hamburg and Cincinnati did he end up as the tournament winner; in Monte Carlo, Montreal and Madrid he lost in the final, while he failed to reach the quarter-finals at the other four Masters tournaments. Nevertheless, Federer defended the top spot in the rankings throughout the season and ended the season in this position for the fourth time in a row after his fourth triumph at the Tennis Masters Cup. Until then, only the Americans Pete Sampras (6×), Jimmy Connors (5×) and John McEnroe (4×) had achieved this.

The next chance to win the Grand Slam came to an end at the start of the 2008 season. Federer was eliminated in the semi-finals of the Australian Open against Novak Đoković. This also broke his streak of ten consecutive finals appearances at Grand Slam tournaments. After the defeat in Melbourne, Federer was unable to win a title until the end of March. This was the first time since 2000 that he had gone the first three months of a season without winning a tournament. On March 7, 2008, Federer announced that he had been suffering from Pfeiffer glandular fever since December of the previous year. At the beginning of April, he won his first title of 2008 in Estoril. During the clay court season, he reached the finals of the Masters Series tournaments in Monte Carlo and Hamburg, where he lost to Rafael Nadal in both cases. Federer also reached his third consecutive final at the French Open, but suffered his third defeat in a row against Nadal. He only managed to win four games in the three-set defeat. Following his defeat in the final in Paris, he secured his second tournament win of the year with his fifth success in Halle. Wimbledon was the sixth time Federer and Nadal had met in the final of a tournament of this category. From 2006 to 2008, they faced each other in every French Open and Wimbledon final, a feat that no other player pairing has ever achieved. After almost five hours of play in the longest Wimbledon final in history, the series of 65 victories on grass and five titles and 40 consecutive victories at Wimbledon came to an end. Federer was beaten 7:9 in the fifth set, leaving him without a win in the first three Grand Slam tournaments of the year for the first time in six years.

Loss and recapture of the world ranking lead (2008-2010)

At the Masters tournament in Cincinnati, he was eliminated in the round of 16, which meant that he was replaced at the top of the world rankings by Nadal after 237 weeks. At the 2008 Olympic Games in Beijing, where he was the flag bearer at the opening ceremony as he had been four years previously, he competed in the singles and doubles alongside Stan Wawrinka. While he was eliminated in the singles quarter-finals against James Blake, he and Wawrinka won the doubles final against the Swedes Simon Aspelin and Thomas Johansson and thus the gold medal.

At the US Open, Federer managed to win the title at a Grand Slam tournament again after three consecutive victories. He beat Andy Murray in three sets in the final. With his fifth consecutive victory at the US Open, he equaled the Open Era record of Pete Sampras and Jimmy Connors and became the first player to win two Grand Slam tournaments five times in a row. During the indoor season, he won his fourth title of the season at the tournament in Basel. At the Masters Series tournament in Madrid, however, he lost to Andy Murray in the semi-finals. The latter also inflicted his second defeat on Federer at the Tennis Masters Cup, meaning that the Swiss failed to reach the group stage for the first time in his seventh participation. Nevertheless, the one victory was enough for him to secure second place in the world rankings at the end of the season.

Federer reached the final at the Australian Open in 2009 and thus had the opportunity to break Pete Sampras' Grand Slam record in the match against Rafael Nadal. However, as in the Wimbledon final, Federer lost to the Spaniard in five sets and more than four hours of play. He only used six of his 19 break opportunities during the match.

He also went untitled at the first two Masters tournaments of the 2009 season. While he lost to Murray in three sets in the semi-finals in Indian Wells, he also failed to reach the final round in Miami against Ðoković. Federer suffered another setback at the start of the clay court season in Monte Carlo when he lost to his doubles partner and friend Stan Wawrinka in two sets in the round of 16. After another semi-final exit against Ðoković in Rome, he managed his first tournament win in seven months in Madrid. He defeated world number one Nadal in two sets in the final, for the first time after five matches without a win in 2008 and 2009, and won his first Masters title since August 2007.

Federer reached the final at the 2009 French Open for the fourth time in a row, having to go the full distance of five sets on his way to the final, both in the round of 16 against Tommy Haas and in the semi-final against Juan Martín del Potro. In the final, he met the Swede Robin Söderling, who had previously inflicted his first defeat at Roland Garros on four-time champion Nadal. Federer won the final 6:1, 7:6 and 6:4, equaling Pete Sampras' record of 14 Grand Slam titles. Federer's success also made him the sixth player in history (after Fred Perry, Don Budge, Rod Laver, Roy Emerson and Andre Agassi) to win all four tournaments of the highest category at least once.

Federer reached the final at Wimbledon in 2009, losing just one set during the tournament. His seventh consecutive appearance in the final was also a new tournament record. He met Andy Roddick for the third time after 2004 and 2005. As in the 2007 and 2008 finals, Federer was forced to go the full distance, but ultimately emerged victorious, winning 5:7, 7:6, 7:6, 3:6 and 16:14, the longest fifth set in a Grand Slam final. He set a new record with his 15th Grand Slam title. As defending champion Nadal had withdrawn due to injury, Federer also regained first place in the world rankings with his sixth Wimbledon success in 46 weeks.

In the subsequent North American hard court season, Federer's streak came to an end after 21 wins in the quarter-finals of Montreal against Jo-Wilfried Tsonga. A week later, he defeated Đoković in the final of Cincinnati and celebrated his fourth win of the season, beating Andy Murray in the semi-finals for the first time in four matches. Federer thus started the US Open once again as the top favorite and, after an interruption of two Grand Slam tournaments, also as the top seed. He reached his sixth US Open final in a row in Flushing Meadows. This was the third time after 2006 and 2007 that he had reached all four Grand Slam finals in one season, setting a new record. As in Melbourne and Wimbledon, the match was only decided in the fifth set. After more than four hours of play, Federer lost 2:6 to Argentina's Juan Martín del Potro in the deciding set, breaking the record streak of 40 consecutive victories at this tournament. At the World Tour Finals at the end of the season, he lost in the semi-finals to the eventual tournament winner Nikolai Davydenko. Nevertheless, the result was enough for him to finish a season at number one in the world rankings for the fifth time, meaning that at this point only Pete Sampras, who has achieved this six times in his career, is ahead of him in this statistic.

The year 2010 began for Federer with a semi-final loss to the eventual tournament winner Davydenko in Doha. At the subsequent Australian Open, he reached his 23rd

Grand Slam semi-final in a row and his eighth Grand Slam final in a row, thanks in part to a successful revenge against Davydenko. He beat Andy Murray in three sets in the final in Melbourne. With his 16th Grand Slam title, Federer equaled Andre Agassi's Open Era record of four Australian Open victories and also won at least one Grand Slam tournament for the eighth season in a row, a feat previously only achieved by Pete Sampras and Björn Borg. After this tournament, Federer's dominance at Grand Slam tournaments, which began in 2004, came to an end.

Federer then suffered from pneumonia and retired early from the Masters tournaments in the USA and at the start of the clay court season. He only made it back to the final at the tournament in Madrid. However, he lost to Nadal in two sets in the rematch of the previous year's final.

Renewed loss of top position (2010-2011)

In the quarter-finals of the French Open, he faced Söderling, whom Federer had beaten in the previous year's final. The Swede got his revenge and Federer's streak of uninterrupted semi-final appearances at Grand Slam tournaments came to an end. Due to Nadal's tournament victory at Roland Garros, he also lost the world number one ranking again to the Spaniard. With a total of 285 weeks at the top of the rankings, he was only one week short of equaling Pete Sampras' record. This ended his streak of eight Grand Slam finals in a row.

Between Wimbledon 2005 and the Australian Open 2010, he reached the final 18 times at nineteen tournaments, only being beaten by Đoković in the semi-finals in Melbourne in 2008.

At the Wimbledon tournament, he was the defending champion and lost to Tomáš Berdych in four sets in the quarter-finals. The defeat meant that Federer lost another place in the world rankings and found himself in third place for the first time in over six years. At his next tournament after Wimbledon, however, he regained position 2 by reaching the final. While he lost the final against Murray, he won his 17th Masters title a week later with a three-set victory over the American Mardy Fish in Cincinnati.

At the 2010 US Open, Federer reached a Grand Slam semi-final again after two recent quarter-final defeats, but lost to Novak Đoković. As a result, he also had to let the Serb pass him in the world rankings. Federer then went on to reach three finals in a row, celebrating tournament victories in Stockholm and at his home tournament in Basel, while he was beaten by Andy Murray in Shanghai. As a result, he once again reached second place in the world rankings and drew level with Sampras in this category with his victory in Stockholm, his 64th tournament win in total.

Federer won the ATP World Tour Finals for the fifth time at the end of the season. He beat Đoković, Murray and Nadal, who were ranked 4th, 3rd and 1st in the world, over the course of the tournament. With his fifth triumph at the final tournament of the season, he drew level with the record winners Lendl and Sampras.

After a successful start to 2011 with a victory in Doha, Federer was defeated by Đoković in the semi-finals at the Australian Open, as he had been at the 2010 US Open. This is the first time Federer has not held a Grand Slam title since Wimbledon 2003.

He then reached the final in Dubai, where he again lost to Đoković, as he did shortly afterwards in the semi-finals of Indian Wells, allowing the Serbian to overtake Federer in the world rankings. After another semi-final defeat to Nadal in Miami, Federer's clay court season began. In his appearances in Monte Carlo, Madrid and Rome, he only reached a semi-final in the Spanish capital, which he lost to Nadal in three sets. At the French Open, he defeated Đoković in the semi-finals after three recent defeats, ending the Serb's winning streak of 43 matches. He lost the final against Nadal in four sets. Federer failed to reach the quarter-finals at Wimbledon, as he had the previous year. In his five-set defeat to Frenchman Jo-Wilfried Tsonga, he squandered a 2-0 set lead for the first time in his Grand Slam career. At the US Open, he reached the quarter-finals of a Grand Slam tournament for the 30th time in a row with a three-set victory in the round of 16 against the Argentinian Juan Monaco. Federer made it through to the semi-finals against Tsonga in three sets. Despite two match points and a 2:0 set lead, he lost to the eventual tournament winner and world number one Đoković. It was the fifth duel in a row in New York since 2007, a record at the Grand Slams. This was the first time Federer had not won a Grand Slam tournament in one season since 2002.

Federer withdrew from the following Masters tournament in Shanghai due to minor injuries. As a result, he dropped to 4th place in the world rankings behind Murray. Federer then celebrated his second tournament success of the year at the Swiss Indoors in Basel; he defeated Japan's Kei Nishikori in the final, who had previously beaten world number one Đoković. A week later, Federer also won the Masters tournament in Paris-Bercy for the first time in his career with a victory over Jo-Wilfried Tsonga in the final.

At the 2011 ATP World Tour Finals, Federer reached his 100th career singles final without losing a match in the group stage, in which he defeated Nadal, among others. By reaching the final, he was also able to return to position 3 in the world rankings at the end of the season. In the final, he met Jo-Wilfried Tsonga, as he had done two weeks earlier in Paris, whom he defeated in three sets. With his sixth success at the final tournament of the season, also his 70th singles title in total, Federer overtook Pete Sampras and Ivan Lendl and is now the sole record winner of the tournament.

Seventh victory at Wimbledon and temporary world number one ranking (2012)

At the beginning of 2012, Federer reached the semi-finals of the Doha tournament, extending his winning streak to 20 victories; however, he withdrew from the semi-final match against Tsonga due to back problems. The Swiss reached the semi-finals at the Australian Open, but was beaten by Nadal in four sets. He played his next tournament in Rotterdam in February, where he reached his first final of the year, which he clearly won in two sets against Juan Martín del Potro. Just two weeks later, he celebrated his next title with a two-set victory over Andy Murray in the Dubai final. At the first Masters tournament of the season in Indian Wells, Federer reached his third final in a row by beating Nadal in the semi-finals. With his 19th success at a Masters tournament in two sets against John Isner, he equaled the record for the most tournament victories in this category. At the Sony Ericsson Open, he was eliminated in the third round against Andy Roddick.

Federer began the clay court season at the Masters tournament in Madrid. At this competition, held on blue clay for the first time, he celebrated his 20th Masters tournament win with a three-set victory over Tomáš Berdych, thus equaling the record for the most Masters titles, which Nadal had improved on in the meantime with a win in Monte Carlo. With his third victory in Madrid, Federer also overtook Nadal in the world rankings and regained second place for the first time since March 2011. A week later, he lost in two sets to Novak Đoković in the semi-finals in Rome and fell back behind Nadal, who won the tournament, in the world rankings.

Federer reached the semi-finals at the French Open, but was once again beaten by Đoković. Over the course of the tournament, he broke the records held by Jimmy Connors for the most match wins at Grand Slam tournaments and the most semi-final appearances at tournaments in this category, surpassing the first-mentioned record.

Federer began the grass court season in Halle, where he reached the final, although he lost in two sets to the German Tommy Haas. Federer then competed at the Wimbledon tournament. Here he overcame a 0:2 set deficit against Frenchman Julien Benneteau in the third round and finally reached his 32nd Grand Slam semi-final, making Federer the sole record holder. As previously in Paris, he met Đoković in the final round, this time beating

him in four sets. Federer thus reached his eighth final at
Wimbledon, another record. In the final, he defeated
Andy Murray, the first Briton to reach the final at
Wimbledon since 1938, 4-6, 7-5, 6-3, 6-4 after trailing in
sets. With his victory, Federer equaled the record of Pete
Sampras and William Renshaw with seven victories at
Wimbledon; it was his 17th Grand Slam title. He also took
the lead in the world rankings for the first time since May
2010, equaling the record of 286 weeks at the top of the
world rankings held by Sampras and becoming the sole
record holder a week later.

At the Olympic Games in London, Federer won his first
individual medal at an Olympic Games with the silver
medal. He was scheduled to carry the Swiss flag for the
third time after Athens and Beijing, but declined the
honor in favor of Stan Wawrinka. In the semi-finals of the
Olympic tennis tournament, which was held at
Wimbledon, he met Juan Martín del Potro, whom he
defeated 19:17 in the third set after almost four and a
half hours of play in the longest three-set match of the
Open Era. The final was a rematch of the Wimbledon final
against Andy Murray, which the Brit won 3-0 in straight
sets.

After canceling his appearance at the Toronto
tournament, Federer began the American hard court
season at the Masters tournament in Cincinnati. There he

won the final in two sets against Đoković and, with his 21st tournament win in this category, set Nadal's record for the most tournament wins at Masters tournaments for the third time. Federer did not give up his serve once during the entire tournament, something he had last achieved in Halle in 2008.

At the subsequent US Open, Federer lost to Tomáš Berdych in four sets in the quarter-finals and thus failed to reach the semi-finals in Flushing Meadows for the first time since 2003. After playing in the Davis Cup for Switzerland against the Netherlands, Federer did not play his next tournament until October in Shanghai. There he reached the last four, where he was beaten by Murray in two sets. At the following home tournament in Basel, he reached his ninth final at this tournament, but lost to del Potro in three sets. As the defending champion, Federer withdrew from the Paris-Bercy tournament a week later. This meant that, after a total of 302 weeks at the top of the world rankings, he would be replaced by Đoković and end 2012 in second place in the rankings.

Federer reached the semi-finals of the final tournament of the season in London despite losing again to del Potro in the group stage. Here he came out on top against Murray in two sets and thus reached his eighth final overall and the third in a row at tournaments of this category. In the final, he faced the new world number one Đoković, to whom he lost 6:7 and 5:7.

Interim fall from the top 5 of the world rankings (2013-2016)

In 2013, Federer reached the semi-finals at the Australian Open, where he lost to Andy Murray in five sets. He reached the quarter-finals at the following tournaments in Rotterdam and Indian Wells, the semi-finals in Dubai and the round of 16 in Madrid. In Rome, he reached his first final of the season, which he clearly lost to Nadal 1:6 and 3:6. At the French Open, he was eliminated in the quarter-finals after losing in three sets to Jo-Wilfried Tsonga. At the Gerry Weber Open in Halle, Federer secured his only title of the season with his sixth victory at this tournament; he won the final against Mikhail Yuzhny in three sets.

Federer made a surprisingly early exit at Wimbledon. He lost in the second round to the unseeded Serhij Stachowskyj 7:6, 6:7, 5:7 and 6:7, ending his streak of 36 consecutive quarter-final appearances at Grand Slam tournaments. He dropped to 5th place in the world rankings and was not in the top 4 for the first time in ten years. He then competed at the Rothenbaum in Hamburg. There he lost to world number 114 Federico Delbonis 6:7 and 6:7 in the semi-finals. In Gstaad he lost his opening match against Daniel Brands. Due to back problems,

Federer was unable to compete at his best at either tournament. As a result, he withdrew from the Canada Masters; in Cincinnati, however, he competed to defend his title. He lost 7-5, 4-6 and 3-6 to Nadal in the quarter-finals, dropping to 7th place in the world rankings behind Juan Martín del Potro and Tomáš Berdych, his worst ranking since October 2002.

Federer lost to Tommy Robredo in the round of 16 at the US Open. The last time he was knocked out so early was in 2003 at the fourth major tournament of the season. His results improved again somewhat in the final weeks of the season. He reached the final at his home tournament in Basel, but was beaten by del Potro in three sets, as he had been the previous year. In his last two tournament appearances in Paris and at the Tour Finals in London, Federer reached the semi-finals in both cases and ended the season at No. 6 in the world rankings. The last time Federer finished a season outside the top 5 was in 2002.

He began the 2014 season by reaching the final in Brisbane. In the final, he lost to Lleyton Hewitt in three sets. At the Australian Open, he defeated Murray in the quarter-finals and then lost to Nadal in three sets in the semi-finals. In Dubai, he defeated Đoković in the semi-finals and Tomáš Berdych in the final, which meant his first tournament victory since Halle the year before and also gave him 4th place in the rankings.

In the next meeting between Federer and Đoković in the Indian Wells final, Federer lost in three sets. At the subsequent Masters in Miami, he lost to Kei Nishikori in the quarter-finals. In Monte Carlo, he reached the final after beating Đoković in the semi-finals, which he lost to his compatriot Stan Wawrinka. At the French Open, he lost in the round of 16 to Ernests Gulbis. At the preparatory tournament for Wimbledon in Halle, he repeated his triumph from the previous year with a victory over Alejandro Falla. He reached the final at Wimbledon, losing to Đoković in a five-set match that lasted almost four hours. At the Masters in Toronto, he reached the final, which he lost to Tsonga 5:7 and 6:7. In Cincinnati, he won his 80th singles title with his victory over David Ferrer in the final.

He reached the semi-finals at the US Open, which he surprisingly lost in three sets to Marin Čilić. Before that, he turned around a 0:2 set deficit against Gaël Monfils for the ninth time in his career; he won the quarter-final 4:6, 3:6, 6:4, 7:5 and 6:2. At the Shanghai Masters, Federer reached his ninth final in 2014, defeating Gilles Simon in two sets, both in tie-breaks, after he had already beaten Đoković in the semi-finals. It was his first title win there and saw him move up to No. 2 in the world rankings. Federer then went on to win the Swiss Indoors with a commanding victory over David Goffin in the final.

At the end of 2014, he took part in the World Tour Finals in London. After defeating Milos Raonic, Kei Nishikori, Andy Murray and Stan Wawrinka, he made it to the final but had to withdraw due to back pain.

2015 began for Federer with a tournament victory in Brisbane. His victory in the final against Milos Raonic was also his 1000th win on the ATP World Tour. Only Ivan Lendl (1071) and Jimmy Connors (1253) had achieved this before him. At the Australian Open, Federer was eliminated in round three against Andreas Seppi. In February, he celebrated his second tournament success of the season in Dubai and his seventh victory at this tournament when he defeated Novak Đoković in the final.

In Indian Wells, he made it to the final, which he lost in three sets to Đoković. Federer's clay court season began with the Masters in Monte Carlo, where he failed to make it past the third round, losing to Gaël Monfils in two sets. He then won the tournament in Istanbul with a victory in the final against Pablo Cuevas. It was his 85th career title and his first tournament win on clay since his triumph in Madrid in 2012. At that tournament, he was seeded No. 1 and lost his opening match against Nick Kyrgios. In Rome, as in Indian Wells, he reached the final against Đoković and again remained winless. Federer reached the quarter-finals of the French Open. He lost the match against his compatriot and eventual tournament winner Stan Wawrinka in three sets.

Federer opened the grass court season with a start at the Gerry Weber Open in Halle. By beating Andreas Seppi in the final, he became only the third player in the Open Era (after Guillermo Vilas and Rafael Nadal) to win a tournament eight times. Federer also reached the final at Wimbledon, his tenth final appearance at this tournament. Once again this season, he lost to Novak Đoković in four sets. He took revenge for this defeat in the final in Cincinnati before the Serb won the final of the US Open again. Federer was unable to defend his title at the Shanghai Masters as he was surprisingly defeated by Spaniard Albert Ramos in his very first match. However, he won the title at the Swiss Indoors Basel again, this time against his long-time rival Nadal. It was his first victory over Nadal in more than three years. At the last Masters tournament in Paris in 2015, Federer was eliminated in the round of 16 against John Isner. He reached the final of the 2015 ATP World Tour Finals, where he again lost to Đoković, whom he had beaten in the group stage.

Federer struggled with injuries in 2016. He only played seven tournaments and failed to win a title for the first time since 2000. He lost to Milos Raonic in the Brisbane final at the start of the season and was beaten once again by Đoković at the Australian Open. Injuries forced him to take a break until the Monte-Carlo Masters. There he played his way through to the quarter-finals before being beaten by Jo-Wilfried Tsonga. In his next two tournament appearances in Rome and Stuttgart, Federer was defeated by the young Austrian Dominic Thiem. He was unable to appear at the French Open, missing out on a Grand Slam tournament for the first time since the 1999 US Open. In Halle, he lost to Alexander Zverev in the semi-finals. At Wimbledon, Federer lost to Milos Raonic in the semi-finals after coming back from a two-set deficit against Marin Čilić in the previous round. He then canceled all further tournaments for 2016 due to persistent knee problems. As a result, he dropped to 16th in the world rankings by the end of the year.

Comeback - first Grand Slam title in five years and eighth Wimbledon triumph (2017)

In Australia, Federer only used the Hopman Cup as preparation for the first Grand Slam tournament of the year, where he won two out of three matches with Belinda Bencic. He won his 18th Grand Slam title at the Australian Open. Only seeded 17th, he first reached the quarter-finals, where he defeated Mischa Zverev in three sets. In the semi-finals, he defeated his compatriot Wawrinka in five sets, who had fought his way back to level the score after losing the first two sets. In the final, he once again met his long-time rival Nadal, whom he had last faced in Melbourne in the 2009 final. Federer was able to take revenge for the five-set defeat back then, again in five sets (6:4, 3:6, 6:1, 3:6, 6:3).

After an early defeat in the round of 16 of the Dubai Championships against qualifier Yevgeny Donskoy, Federer managed to win the Paribas Open in Indian Wells in his fourth tournament start of the year, where he defeated Wawrinka in two sets in the final. This put Federer back at number 6 in the world rankings. After a tight semi-final against Nick Kyrgios in three sets, each decided in a tie-break, Federer won this title and the so-called Sunshine Double consisting of Indian Wells and Miami for the third time with a smooth two-set victory over Nadal in the Miami final. As a result, Federer improved to 4th place in the world rankings.

Federer decided to forgo the clay court season and only returned to tournaments for the grass court season. At the Mercedes Cup in Stuttgart, he was knocked out in the round of 16 by Tommy Haas, but then won his ninth title at the tournament in Halle in the final against Alexander Zverev, against whom he had been knocked out in the semi-finals the previous year. Federer won his 19th Grand Slam title at Wimbledon and reached the final for the third time after 2006 and 2008 without losing a set and for the eleventh time overall, winning five tie-breaks without having to fend off a break point. In the final, he clearly defeated Marin Čilić in three sets (6:3, 6:1, 6:4) to win the grass court tournament for the first time without losing a set. He thus overtook Britain's William Renshaw and the US American Pete Sampras, who had each won the Wimbledon singles final seven times. At 35 years and 342 days, Federer was the oldest Wimbledon finalist since Ken Rosewall in 1974. His success in the final makes him the oldest winner of the tournament in the Open Era.

He then took a short break from the tournament until the Masters in Montreal. There he missed out on his sixth title in the sixth final of the year against Alexander Zverev in two sets. The following week in Cincinnati, he would have had the chance to return to the top of the world rankings with a tournament win, but had to cancel his participation due to back pain. At the US Open, he was eliminated in the quarter-finals against Juan Martín del Potro. Two weeks later, he won the 2017 Laver Cup as a member of the European team and played a doubles match alongside Rafael Nadal for the first time, which the pair won 6:4, 1:6, [10:5] against Sam Querrey and Jack Sock; his singles victories against Querrey (6:4, 6:2) and Nick Kyrgios (4:6, 7:6, [11:9]) were also crucial contributions to the European team's 15:9 win. He then won the tournaments in Shanghai and Basel in succession. At the end of the season, Federer reached the semi-finals of the ATP Finals, where he was somewhat surprisingly beaten by David Goffin. With a total of seven tournament wins from eleven tournaments, 2017 was Federer's most successful year in the last ten years - he only won more titles in the seasons from 2004 to 2007. However, it was not enough for first place in the world rankings, as Rafael Nadal also won two Grand Slam tournaments this year and scored more points in the other two than Federer, who missed out on Paris. Federer had the chance to become number one several times, but stuck to his strategy of taking longer breaks after tournaments and playing fewer tournaments overall.

20th Grand Slam title

Federer successfully defended his title at the Australian Open at the beginning of 2018, winning his 20th Grand Slam title and equaling the record held by Roy Emerson and Novak Đoković with his sixth victory in Melbourne. Contrary to his original plans for the season, he decided to enter the tournament in Rotterdam in mid-February as he had the opportunity to knock Rafael Nadal, who had been injured in the meantime, off the top of the world rankings. He succeeded in doing so by beating Robin Haase in the quarter-finals. In the final of the tournament, he beat world number three Grigor Dimitrov in two sets 6:2, 6:2. On February 19, 2018, after an interruption of more than five years, Federer became the oldest number 1 in history. After losing the final to Juan Martin del Potro at the Indian Wells tournament (4:6, 7:6, 6:7) and then losing in the second round to Thanasi Kokkinakis at the Miami tournament (6:3, 3:6, 6:7) had been unable to defend his points as last year's winner and had therefore temporarily lost the world number one ranking to Rafael Nadal, he set the stage for his return to the number one ranking by reaching the final and then winning his first final against Milos Raonic (6:4, 7:6) at the Stuttgart tournament. Prior to that, Federer had missed out on the clay court season for the third time in a row. In Halle, he reached the final for the twelfth time, but lost it to Borna Ćorić in three sets 6:7, 6:3, 2:6. At Wimbledon, Federer competed as the defending champion, but surprisingly lost to Kevin Anderson in the quarter-finals in five sets 6:2, 7:6, 5:7, 4:6, 11:13 after more than four hours of play. This was the third time he lost a match at a Grand Slam tournament after leading 2:0 in sets. He reached the 150th final of his career in Cincinnati, but lost it in two sets to Novak Đoković, his first defeat in the final in Ohio. At the US Open, he lost to John Millman in four sets in the round of 16. Federer had considerable problems with the high temperatures and high humidity in this match, Millman coped better with it. In Shanghai, Federer lost 4:6, 4:6 to Borna Ćorić in the semi-finals. As Novak Đoković won the tournament, Federer dropped to third place in the world rankings. At his home tournament in Basel, he won the title for the ninth time when he beat Marius Copil 7:6, 6:4 in the final, this victory was the 99th title of his career. At the Masters in Paris, he narrowly lost to Novak Đoković in the semi-finals in three sets, 6:7, 7:5, 6:7. He then took part in the ATP Finals for the 16th time in total. He lost the first match against Kei Nishikori, but won the next two matches against Dominic Thiem and Kevin Anderson in two sets and then met Alexander Zverev in the semi-finals, losing 5:7 and 6:7. Federer thus ended the season in third place in the world rankings.

100th title of the career (2019)

At the start of the 2019 season, he won the Hopman Cup in Perth for the third time with Belinda Bencic. Federer was unable to defend his title at the Australian Open, losing to Stefanos Tsitsipas in four tight sets in the round of 16, which also snapped his streak of 17 consecutive victories in Melbourne. With his eighth title in Dubai, he became the second player in the Open Era after Jimmy Connors to reach 100 tournament wins in singles. He defeated Stefanos Tsitsipas in two sets in the final. He reached the final of the Indian Wells Masters for the ninth time, but lost in three sets to Dominic Thiem, who won his first Masters title. At the Miami Masters, he won his 101st title with a two-set victory over John Isner. It was his fourth title in Miami and his 28th Masters triumph in his fiftieth final, and at the Masters in Madrid he played a tournament on clay for the first time since 2016, where he lost to Dominic Thiem in three sets after two wins in the quarter-finals. He also reached the quarter-finals at the subsequent tournament in Rome, but Federer did not play his match against Stefanos Tsitsipas due to a leg injury. He then returned to the French Open for the first time since 2015, reaching the semi-finals there again after seven years, which Federer clearly lost in three sets to the eventual winner Rafael Nadal. He won the tournament in Halle for the tenth time after a two-set victory against David Goffin, making him the second player in the Open

Era after Nadal to reach the number of ten victories at a tournament.

Federer reached the final at Wimbledon for the twelfth time, but lost it for the third time against Novak Đoković in five sets 6:7, 6:1, 6:7, 6:4, 12:13. With a playing time of 4 hours and 57 minutes, it was the longest Wimbledon final in history, and also the first time that a tie-break was played in the deciding set in a singles match. He had previously achieved his 100th victory at Wimbledon by beating Kei Nishikori in the quarter-finals, something no other player had ever achieved before. At the US Open, he lost to Grigor Dimitrov in five sets in the quarter-finals. In Basel, he won his tenth title at this tournament without dropping a set, winning there for the third time in a row. He reached the semi-finals of the ATP Finals for the 16th time in total, but lost there to Stefanos Tsitsipas in two sets. Prior to that, he defeated Novak Đoković in the group stage for the first time since 2015. He finished the season in third place in the rankings once again.

Knee injury problems and end of career (2020-2022)

In 2020, Federer reached his 15th semi-final at the Australian Open, where he clearly lost to Đoković in three sets. He had previously won his 100th match at this tournament against John Millman in the third round. On February 20, 2020, Federer announced that he had undergone surgery on his right knee the day before. He subsequently canceled his participation in all tournaments up to and including the French Open and planned his comeback for the grass court season in June. In the summer, however, he had to have another operation on the same knee, which meant the end of the season. In Federer's absence, Rafael Nadal equaled his record with his 20th Grand Slam victory at the French Open 2020, which was postponed due to the COVID-19 pandemic.

In March 2021, Federer made his comeback in Doha after a 14-month break. After defeating Daniel Evans in his first match, he lost to Nikolos Bassilashvili in the next round. He reached the round of 16 at the French Open, but did not play Matteo Berrettini in order to rest up for the upcoming grass court season. At Wimbledon, Federer reached his 18th quarter-final at this tournament, which he surprisingly lost to Hubert Hurkacz 4:6, 6:7, 0:6. It was his first three-set defeat in London since 2002. After this tournament, he underwent another knee operation, ending his season prematurely.

Federer played the last official match of his career on September 23, 2022: at the Laver Cup in London, he and Rafael Nadal competed in the doubles for Team Europe against the Americans Jack Sock and Frances Tiafoe. Federer and Nadal lost 6:4, 6:7 (2:7), [9:11].

Davis Cup

Roger Federer has a record of 52 wins and 20 defeats in 26 Davis Cup matches (40:8 in singles and 12:10 in doubles). He has been a regular member of the Swiss team since 1999 and led his country to the title in 2014 and to the semi-finals of the competition in 2003. In 1999, 2001 and 2004, Federer reached the quarter-finals of the competition with the Swiss team.

Since the 2005 season, Federer has concentrated mainly on his singles career and did not take part in his country's first-round matches from 2005 to 2007, whereupon Switzerland failed in the first round in each case. However, Federer subsequently took part in the qualifying round in order to prevent his country from being relegated from the World Group. While this was successful in 2005 and 2006, Switzerland lost 3-2 to the Czech Republic in the relegation round in 2007, despite Federer's two successes in the singles, and was thus no longer represented in the World Group in 2008 for the first time in 16 years.

In September 2008, the Swiss team with Federer and Wawrinka achieved immediate promotion back to the World Group with a win against Belgium. After Federer again missed Switzerland's first round match in 2009, in which the team lost to the USA, he was back in the team in the relegation match against Italy in September. With two singles victories, Federer helped to prevent

Switzerland from being relegated from the World Group again.

Federer did not play a Davis Cup match in 2010, whereupon the Swiss team was relegated to the European Group again after 2007. In 2011, Federer took part in Switzerland's match against Portugal in the European Group and contributed to the Swiss team qualifying for the promotion round to the World Group with two singles victories. Here, Switzerland beat Australia 3:2, with Federer again contributing two singles victories, to advance to the World Group.

In February 2012, Federer took part in Switzerland's first round match against the USA for the first time since 2004. He lost both his opening singles match and his doubles match alongside Wawrinka, meaning that Switzerland were already the losers after the doubles match. However, Federer helped the team to stay in the World Group with two singles victories in the relegation match against the Netherlands in September 2012.

In 2014, Federer was back in the Swiss team after a one-year break and helped them reach the next round in the first round against Serbia with one singles win and in the quarter-finals against Kazakhstan with two singles wins. In the semi-final against Italy, he contributed two singles wins to the team's victory, which meant that Switzerland reached the final of the competition for the second time in its Davis Cup history after 1992. In the final against France, Federer first lost his opening singles match against Gaël Monfils in three sets, but then won both the doubles match alongside Wawrinka, who had previously won his opening singles match, and his second singles match against Richard Gasquet, which meant that the Swiss team were Davis Cup winners ahead of time.

With 52 wins, Federer is in first place in his country's all-time ranking. His winning percentage is by far the most successful of all players with more than 20 appearances.

International Premier Tennis League (IPTL)

Roger Federer played as one of the top stars in the newly founded International Premier Tennis League and competed in this new format in Asia as part of the *Indian Aces* team. Together with his teammates Gaël Monfils, Ana Ivanović, Sania Mirza, Rohan Bopanna and former players Fabrice Santoro and Pete Sampras, he won the inaugural title on December 13, 2014.

Show fights

Immediately after the Tennis Masters Cup, Federer faced Rafael Nadal in an exhibition match in Seoul on November 21, 2006. Federer beat the Mallorcan 6:3, 3:6 and 6:3.

In May 2007, Federer met Rafael Nadal again in the "Battle of Surfaces" in Palma. In front of 7,000 spectators, the two duelled on a court with different surfaces. On one side of the net, the Swiss player's favorite court, grass, and on the other, Nadal's preferred clay. Nadal won 7:5, 4:6 and 7:6 (12:10) in the sold-out Palma Arena. Federer played a much-noticed exhibition series in November 2007, when he competed against Pete Sampras in three exhibitions. While the Swiss easily won the opening match in Seoul 6:3 and 6:4, Sampras put up more resistance in match number two in Kuala Lumpur and forced Federer into tie-breaks twice. Federer prevailed 7:6 (8:6) and 7:6 (7:5). Federer only lost 6:7 (8:10) and 4:6 to the ten years older American in their last duel in Macau.

On March 10, 2008, Federer defeated the American in three sets 6:3, 6:7 (4:7) and 7:6 (8:6) in another meeting with Sampras. The match was played in front of 19,000 spectators in New York's Madison Square Garden. Federer took part in the *Showdown of Champions* on November 18, 2008. He defeated James Blake 7:6 in the first match and then lost 5:7 to John McEnroe and James Blake in the following doubles match with Björn Borg.

In March 2010, Federer and Sampras played a show doubles match in Indian Wells against Rafael Nadal and Andre Agassi in aid of the earthquake victims in Haiti. Federer/Sampras won the "Hit for Haiti" event 8:6. On December 21 and 22, 2010, Federer and Nadal played two exhibition matches, the first in Zurich and the second in

Madrid. Each match was played to two sets won. The proceeds went to the respective charity funds of the two rivals. In his "Match for Africa", Federer made the most of his home advantage and defeated Nadal 4:6, 6:3 and 6:3 in Zurich, but lost 7:6 (7:3), 3:6 and 1:6 to Nadal in Madrid.

Four years later, on December 21, 2014, a new edition of the "Match for Africa" took place in Zurich's Hallenstadion, this time against Stan Wawrinka. Federer won the duel against his Davis Cup partner 7:6, 6:4.

On January 12, 2015, Federer played his first major public match in the Fast4 format against Lleyton Hewitt in Sydney. Federer won 4:3 (5:3), 2:4, 3:4 (3:5) 4:0, 4:2.

In November 2019, Federer traveled to five Latin American countries (Argentina, Chile, Colombia, Mexico and Ecuador) within seven days, where he played one match each against German Alexander Zverev - the players share their management company. Due to social unrest and a curfew, the match in Colombia's capital Bogotà was canceled. Federer received an estimated fee of 10 million dollars for the five matches. In Mexico City, Federer and Zverev played in front of 41,157 in the "Plaza de Toros", a bullring. They set a new world record for a tennis match. Federer was heavily criticized for his trip to countries plagued by social unrest.

Trainer

- *1989-1994:* Adolf Kacovský (Switzerland, now Czech Republic) had a significant influence on Federer's game during his childhood. Kacovský worked with him as coach of the tennis club TC Old Boys Basel until Federer moved to Ecublens in 1995.

- *1991-1995, 1997-2000:* Peter Carter (Australia) also coached Federer during his time with the Old Boys Basel. After Federer's switch to the international tour, Carter became his association coach. Carter remained a close advisor to Federer even after he left the association.

- *1995-1997:* Federer spent the years 1995-1997 at the Swiss national training center in Ecublens, where he was promoted by the federation to enter the international junior tour.

- *2000-2003:* Peter Lundgren (Sweden) coached Federer partly as a federation coach before 2000 and became the Swiss's private coach after the separation from the federation. The separation followed after the 2003 season.

- *2004:* Federer played 2004 without a coach.

- *2005-2007:* Tony Roche (Australia) coached Federer part-time at important tournaments from 2005 to 2007, before parting ways in May 2007. Federer spent the rest of the year without a coach.

- *2008:* In April, Roger Federer temporarily hired the then 55-year-old Spaniard José Higueras to prepare for the clay court season. The collaboration continued until the 2008 US Open. From fall 2008, Federer worked without a coach again.

- *2010-2013:* Federer employed Paul Annacone (USA) as his coach in August. After Federer's retirement from the 2013 Shanghai Masters, the collaboration was terminated.

- *2014-2015:* Federer's "childhood idol" Stefan Edberg (Sweden) was co-coach alongside Severin Lüthi, who has accompanied him on the tour since 2007. Federer announced his separation from Edberg at the beginning of December 2015.

- *2016-2022:* From January 2016 until the end of his career in September 2022, Federer was supported alongside Lüthi by Ivan Ljubičić (Croatia) as co-coach, who had already coached

Canadian tennis pro Milos Raonic from 2013 to 2015.

Supplier

For most of his career, Federer had a contract with Nike for his shoes and clothing. After the 2008 Wimbledon tournament, Nike made him a personalized advertising medium with its own logo. In July 2018, Federer played in clothes from his new Japanese sponsor Uniqlo for the first time.

Playing style

Roger Federer is considered the most versatile player in tennis today and also one of the best all-rounders in the history of professional tennis. In 2007, American *Tennis Magazine ranked the* Swiss player among the best players of today's tennis generation in a total of seven out of eleven categories when listing the best players in certain areas of the game. He was also ranked among the best players in tennis history in four areas. This versatile and varied game not only enabled Federer to be successful on different court surfaces, but also made him the dominant player of his generation. His all-round game prevailed over more one-sided players of his generation such as Andy Roddick (serve) or Lleyton Hewitt (footwork and return game). However, it should also be mentioned that the continuous standardization of court surfaces offers a decisive advantage for the style of play of all-round players.

In terms of his basic structure, Federer belongs to the type of player who is predominant in today's professional tennis and who essentially plays from the baseline. Although Federer has also worked on his net game, especially in the years under his coach Tony Roche, he still wins the majority of his points by hitting from the baseline. The most spectacular and successful shot in

Federer's game is his forehand, which Tennis Magazine has described as the best forehand in the history of the sport. According to expert Skidelsky, the secret of his forehand lies in his racket position, the *modified eastern grip*, which allows him to play every ball. Because of its speed, accuracy and reliability, Federer usually uses his forehand to end a rally directly or to force his opponent into a decisive error. Compared to the forehand, Federer's backhand is seen as his weaker side. Federer uses his backhand to a large extent to prepare a winning shot. Federer often uses the backhand slice, especially on returns, to force his opponent into a defensive situation. Forcing Federer to play with his backhand is one of the most tried and tested tactics to put the Swiss in trouble. High-jumping shots on the backhand were therefore one of five possible ways to beat Federer suggested by Time magazine in 2007 following interviews with various tennis experts and players.

Although Federer's strong forehand usually takes up the most space in descriptions of his style of play, his defensive play and especially his footwork and movement on the court are also considered an important factor in his success. Tennis Magazine, for example, also described Federer's footwork as the best in the history of the sport. The conditioning coach Pierre Paganini, with whom the Swiss has been working since the end of the 2000 season, is regarded as a key figure in the development of

Federer's movement sequences on the tennis court. Paganini trains with Federer in the areas of athleticism, footwork and strength training. The targeted work in these areas enables Federer to be particularly quick on short running routes, so that he can run into opponents' shots faster than most other players and return them with much more considered shots. This opens up the opportunity for the Swiss to go on the offensive again himself from sometimes very heavy pressure or to win points directly.

Other areas of Roger Federer's game tend to be mentioned in passing in most analyses. For example, the Swiss player's serve is not considered one of his greatest strengths, but Federer has one of the most variable serves on the ATP Tour. In fact, Federer hits far fewer aces and service winners than the best servers in tennis today. Nevertheless, Federer has improved significantly in this area in recent years. At the end of his career, he had hit a total of 11,478 aces, the third most on the tour. He has therefore continuously increased his average number of aces per match in recent years. Since 2002, Federer has also been among the top ten players in this statistic for the year in question, winning around 77% of his first serves. He has also won 88.8% of his service games, only four players have a better rate.

Although net play has become less important in world tennis in recent years, Federer not only uses the net regularly on fast surfaces to convert good serves directly, but also frequently on slow surfaces such as clay to shorten run-intensive baseline duels. However, Federer is not regarded as one of the best volley players, especially in historical comparison. Although Tennis Magazine named Federer as one of the best current players in this area, Federer was regularly passed at the net by the Spaniard, especially in his numerous clay court duels against Rafael Nadal. The typical clay court shots such as stop or lob shots were also not part of the Swiss player's frequent repertoire for a long time. However, Federer also steadily improved with these shots. On the way to his French Open victory in 2009 and throughout the rest of the season, he regularly and effectively incorporated the stop ball into his game.

In addition to the pure level of playing ability, the mental aspect is also a decisive factor in tennis, especially at Grand Slam tournaments. In this context, it is remarkable that Federer, who was considered a very vocal and hot-headed player in his younger years, changed his demeanor on the court considerably early on in his professional career. Even in tight match situations, Federer rarely shows any emotion, making it difficult for his opponents to assess his actual condition. Federer is also known for playing his best tennis in crucial situations.

Proof of this is his strong tie-break record (Federer ranks first in the statistics of players with more than 100 tie-breaks, having won around 66% of them) and the percentage of break chances he has fended off (Federer ranked first among ATP players here in the 2006 season with 70%).

All of Federer's playing skills, coupled with his almost unprecedented success rate in recent years, have led to many players writing off their matches against Federer as lost even before they actually take place. This is an observation that Time magazine also addressed in its article on ways to beat Federer. David Nalbandian, who won a total of eight duels against Federer, believes that many players would have a better chance against Federer if they went into their matches against the Swiss with a different motivation.

In 2015, Federer attracted attention in the tennis world with a new return technique in which he returns the ball as early as possible after his opponent's serve in order to give them less time for their next shot. The shot became known as *Sabr* (Sneak Attack by Roger).

Honors & awards

Federer was named Player of the Year by the International Tennis Federation (ITF) in 2004, 2005, 2006, 2007 and 2009. He was also voted Laureus World Sportsman of the Year five times (2005, 2006, 2007, 2008 and 2018) and won the PAP European Sportsman of the Year award five times as well as the title of the same name from the Union of European Sports Journalists (UEPS) six times, which no athlete before him has ever achieved. He was named international "Champion des champions" four times by the French sports newspaper *L'Équipe* (2005, 2006, 2007, 2017). In the same years, he was voted World Sportsman of the Year by the Italian sports newspaper *La Gazzetta dello Sport.* Federer was also voted BBC Overseas Sports Personality of the Year four times (2004, 2006, 2007, 2017) and received a total of ten ESPY Awards, of which he was voted best tennis player nine times (2005-2010, 2017-2019). In 2018, he received the award for Comeback of the Year at the Laureus Awards, making him the record holder at the Laureus World Sports Awards with a total of six awards.

Between 2003 and 2021, Federer was voted *Fans' Favorite* in an online poll at the ATP Awards. Federer has also received the *Stefan Edberg Sportsmanship Award a* total of 13 times, an award for fairness and exemplary behavior both on and off the court. At the end of 2017, Federer was honored with the *Comeback Player of the Year* award at the ATP Awards.

In his home country, Federer was voted Swiss Sportsman of the Year seven times (2003, 2004, 2006, 2007, 2012, 2014, 2017). He also won Team of the Year in 2008 with Stan Wawrinka and in 2014 with the Davis Cup team (together with Wawrinka, Michael Lammer and Marco Chiudinelli). In 2003 he was Swiss of the Year. In 2020, he was voted the best Swiss athlete of the last 70 years. In 2022, Federer was awarded the honorary prize for his career at the Swiss Sports Awards, which was last presented in 2009.

In 2009, Federer was named "Ehrespalebärglemer" in Basel.

In 2007, Swiss Post was the first living personality to dedicate a special stamp to Federer. In September 2009, Austrian Post announced that it would also be honoring Federer in 2010 by issuing a special stamp.

At the suggestion of the director of the Halle tournament, Ralf Weber, part of Haller *Weststraße* was renamed *Roger-Federer-Allee* on the occasion of the Gerry Weber Open 2012. On April 21, 2016, a new street in Biel was named Roger-Federer-Allee after him.

On November 24, 2017, it was announced that the University of Basel had awarded Roger Federer an honorary doctorate. The Faculty of Medicine is thus recognizing his contribution to enhancing the international reputation of Basel and Switzerland. The Basel-born athlete has a role model function "in which he encourages many people worldwide to exercise more and thus makes an important contribution to health promotion"

The Patrouille Suisse, the Swiss Air Force's aerobatic squadron, flies a "Roger Federer" formation figure during demonstrations, in which the six F5 Tigers are positioned in the shape of a tennis racket as they fly past.

In 2021, the Basel transport company dedicated a streetcar to Roger Federer called the Federer Express, decorated with photos of him, which he inaugurated in person.

Records

Grand Slam tournaments

- Roger Federer holds the record for the most Grand Slam quarter-finals reached (58), while his records for the most finals reached (31) and semi-finals (46) were beaten by Novak Đoković. With 20 Grand Slam titles, he is in third place behind Đoković (24) and Rafael Nadal (22). In 2009, he became the record winner in this tournament category with his 15th Grand Slam title at Wimbledon, until his record was surpassed by Nadal in 2022.

- Federer is one of eight players to have won all four Grand Slam tournaments in their career. Alongside Andre Agassi, Rafael Nadal and Novak Đoković, he is the only player to have won these tournaments on three different surfaces.

- Federer is the only player to win three Grand Slam tournaments in two consecutive years (2006, 2007). In 2007, he also became the first player to defend the three titles from the previous year (Australian Open, Wimbledon & US Open).

- Federer is the first player to win three different Grand Slam tournaments at least five times (Australian Open six times, US Open five times and Wimbledon eight times). The Swiss is also the only player to win two different Grand Slam tournaments five times in a row (Wimbledon 2003-2007, US Open 2004-2008).

- Federer holds the record for the most consecutive years (4) with at least two Grand Slam victories in a season (2004-2007).

- Federer has reached at least one Grand Slam final in 15 seasons (2003-2012, 2014, 2015, 2017-2019), which is also a record, but Nadal and Đoković have since equaled it.

- The Swiss holds the records for the most consecutive quarter-final (36, Wimbledon 2004 to French Open 2013) and semi-final appearances (23, Wimbledon 2004 to Australian Open 2010) at tournaments in this category. He also reached the final ten times in a row (Wimbledon 2005 to US Open 2007), making Federer the only player to reach all four Grand Slam finals in two consecutive years (2006 and 2007). Between Wimbledon 2005 and the Australian Open 2010, he reached 18 of 19 possible finals, only missing out on the final at the Australian Open 2008.

Between Wimbledon 2003 and the Australian Open 2010, he won 25 quarter-finals in a row.

- Federer is the only player to reach all four Grand Slam finals in three seasons (2006, 2007, 2009).

- At the 2007 Australian Open, Federer became the first player since Björn Borg in Paris in 1980 to win a Grand Slam tournament without dropping a set. By winning the first four rounds of the subsequent French Open without dropping a set, he equaled John McEnroe's record from 1984 for winning eleven consecutive matches without dropping a set at Grand Slam tournaments. He also set another record by winning 36 Grand Slam sets in a row. In 2017, he won another Grand Slam tournament at Wimbledon without dropping a set.

- With his first-round victory over Tobias Kamke at the 2012 French Open, Federer equaled the record held by Jimmy Connors for the most match wins at Grand Slam tournaments (233). With his subsequent second-round victory over Adrian Ungur, he became the sole record holder with 234 wins. Federer then extended the record to 369 wins.

- In the 2009 Wimbledon final (5:7, 7:6, 7:6, 3:6, 16:14), Federer and Roddick set several other records: the largest number of games in a Grand Slam final (77) and the largest number of games in the final set of a Grand Slam final (30). Federer also hit more aces than any other player in a previous Grand Slam final (50).

- Since January 2020, Roger Federer is the only player to have won at least 100 matches at two different tournaments (Wimbledon & Australian Open).

- Federer is also the only tennis player to have won the title in each of his first seven finals at Grand Slam tournaments.

- Federer was seeded No. 1 at a Grand Slam tournament 18 times in a row between Paris 2004 and Wimbledon 2008.

- Federer has been the oldest winner of the Grand Slam tournament at Wimbledon in the Open Era since 2017. This makes him the second oldest winner of a Grand Slam tournament in the Open Era after Ken Rosewall, who won the Australian Open in 1972 at the age of 37.

- With eight individual titles at Wimbledon (2003-2007, 2009, 2012, 2017), he is the sole record holder at this tournament.

- With five singles victories at the US Open (2004-2008), Federer is the record winner of the tournament in the Open Era alongside Jimmy Connors and Pete Sampras.

ATP Finals and previous events

- Federer, together with Đoković, holds the record for the most tournament wins at the season-ending tournament with six victories.

- He is also the record holder for the most finals (10) and semi-finals (16) reached.

- Federer qualified for the season-ending tournament 14 times in a row (2002-2015), which is also a record. He also holds the record for the most participations overall (17).

- On November 6, 2012, Federer won his 40th match at end-of-season tournaments, surpassing Ivan Lendl's previous record. Federer has since extended this record to 59 victories.

- In 2005, he was the first player to defeat his opponent in a match at the Tennis Masters Cup with a score of 6:0 and 6:0. His opponent was

Gastón Gaudio in the semi-finals of the tournament.

- Federer was the only player to win the tournament five times without losing in round-robin fashion.

ATP Tour Masters 1000

- Federer also holds important records in the tournament series, which was introduced in 1990. In 2012 and 2013, he briefly shared the record for the most tournament wins in the Masters Series with Nadal; he is now in third place in this ranking with 28 tournament wins behind Novak Đoković (38 wins) and Nadal (36).

- In 2005, Federer became the first player ever to win four tournaments in this category in one season. He achieved this again the following season. This mark was later also reached by Rafael Nadal in 2005 and surpassed by Novak Đoković in 2011 and Rafael Nadal in 2013 with five successes and even by Đoković in 2015 with six successes in one year.

- Federer held the record for the most finals appearances in one season (6; 2006). The Swiss held this record together with Novak Đoković, who also achieved this in the 2011 season, and

Rafael Nadal (2013). In the 2015 season, Đoković improved the record to eight final appearances.

- In addition to the eight different tournaments that Federer has won, he has also reached the final at two other tournaments in this category (Monte Carlo, Rome). This participation in the finals of ten different Masters tournaments, including all nine on the current tour calendar, also represents a record. Federer holds this record together with Rafael Nadal. Both have reached the final in all tournaments of the Masters series with the exception of the Stuttgart Masters, which was only held until 2001.

- Federer was the first player to win the double from the tournaments in Indian Wells and Miami twice in a row (2005 and 2006). Novak Đoković even managed this three times in 2014, 2015 and 2016.

- At the four North American tournaments (Indian Wells, Miami, Canada and Cincinnati), Federer was the third player after Andre Agassi and Michael Chang to enter each of the four winners' lists at least once. He and Đoković were the only players to win each of these tournaments more than once. In 2005, he was the only player to date to win the Indian Wells, Miami and Cincinnati tournaments in one season.

- At the 2012 tournament in Cincinnati, Federer became the first player in the history of the tournament series to win a tournament without losing a set or his own serve, and in Cincinnati 2015 he was the only one to do so for a second time.

- At the 2014 tournament in Cincinnati, Federer became the first player to surpass the 300-win mark at tournaments in this category.

- Roger Federer won the Miami Masters in 2019 at the age of 37 years and 7 months. This made him the oldest player to win a tournament in the Masters tournament series.

World ranking list

- Federer holds or has held numerous records in both the world rankings and the ATP Champions Race. For example, he set the record for the most points at the end of the season in both ranking systems. In 2006, he scored 1,674 points in the Champions Race and 8,370 in the world rankings (equivalent to 15,745 in the revised rankings since 2009). This score was also the record for the highest number of points ever achieved by a player in the world rankings in one year. In September 2015, Novak Đoković surpassed this mark with 16,145 points. Federer was also the first player to exceed the 7,000 and 8,000 point marks since the rating system was introduced.

- On February 26, 2007, Federer broke Jimmy Connors' previous record for the number of consecutive weeks at the top of the world rankings (160 weeks, 1974-1977) and on August 27, 2007, he also broke Steffi Graf's record of 186 consecutive weeks. Federer extended this record to 237 weeks by August 18, 2008. Federer (2005-2007) and Connors (1975, 1976, 1978) are the only players to have held the top spot for three complete calendar years, with Federer the only one to do so three years in a row.

- Following his Wimbledon victory in 2012, Federer set Pete Sampras' record for the most weeks at the top of the world rankings on July 9, 2012 with 286 weeks. One week later, he became the sole record holder. In the following four months, he extended this record to 302 weeks, and five and a half years later, after his return to the tennis throne on February 20, to 310 weeks. This record was first set by Novak Đoković on March 1, 2021 and then surpassed the following week.

- Alongside Ivan Lendl (1989), Rafael Nadal (2010, 2013, 2017, 2019) and Novak Đoković (2014, 2018, 2020), Federer is one of four players to finish a season as the top-ranked player again after losing the number 1 spot at the end of the year. After finishing 2004-2007 at No. 1, Federer ended 2008 as runner-up, but returned to the top spot in 2009.

- With his victory at the tournament in Rotterdam on February 19, 2018, Federer became the oldest number 1 since the introduction of the world rankings at 36 years and 195 days. This record had previously been held by Andre Agassi at 33 years and 131 days. Federer extended his record again to 36 years and 314 days when he returned to the top of the world rankings on June 18, 2018 after temporarily losing the top spot twice.

- At 14 years and 136 days (February 2, 2004 to June 18, 2018), he holds the record for the longest period of time between the first and last period as number 1. The gap of 5 years and 106 days (November 4, 2012 to February 19, 2018) between the last two periods at the top is also a record.

- Federer holds various long-term records in the world rankings. Between November 17, 2003 and

July 4, 2010, he was listed in the top 2 of the rankings for 346 consecutive weeks. He is the player with the most weeks in the top 3 (750), top 5 (859) and top 10 (968). He also finished the most years in the top 3 (15), top 5 (16) and top 10 (18).

- He spent 1147 consecutive weeks in the Top 50 (June 12, 2000 to June 6, 2022) and 1187 consecutive weeks in the Top 100 (October 11, 1999 to June 20, 2022) - both are record streaks.

Winning streaks

In his career to date, Federer has achieved a series of winning streaks in various areas.

- Federer celebrated 24 consecutive victories against opponents from the top 10 of the world rankings (2003-2005).

- Federer also holds the Open Era record for the most consecutive finals wins (24, the streak ended in 2005).

- The Swiss holds the records for the longest winning streaks on grass and hard courts, with 56 victories on hard courts (2005-2006) and 65 consecutive victories on grass (2003-2008).

Other records

- On October 30, 2017, Federer overtook the previous record holder Novak Đoković with 109,853,682 US dollars in prize money won, the first professional tennis player to pass the 100 million dollar mark. Federer had already taken the lead in this ranking in October 2008, but was overtaken by Đoković for a year and a half in April 2016. With two victories in the first two group matches at the ATP Finals in London in November 2017, he achieved a total of 110,235,682 dollars, breaking the record held by professional golfer Tiger Woods (110,061,012 dollars). However, Federer was overtaken again in 2018 by the resurgent Đoković. From 2006 to 2010, Federer also held the record for the highest prize money in a season.

- Alongside Rod Laver, Roger Federer is one of only two players to have won ten or more tournaments in three consecutive years. These 34 singles titles won in the years 2004-2006 are another record.

- With a win rate of 94.3% and a tournament win rate of 69.4%, Federer can also boast two all-time high rates for a period of three years.

- Reaching the final in 16 out of 17 tournaments played (94.1%, 2006 season) was also a new record.

- Federer holds the record for the most tournament victories on hard courts (71) and on grass (19) in the Open Era, as well as the most matches won on both surfaces. With a total of 103 tournament victories on all surfaces, he is in second place behind Jimmy Connors (109 wins). With a total of 157 finals reached, he is also behind Jimmy Connors (164). His 1251 victories and 1526 matches played are only surpassed by Connors.

- The 86.88% win rate on grass is a record in the Open Era.

- The London 2012 Olympic semi-final, which Federer won against Juan Martín del Potro 3:6, 7:6 (7:5) and 19:17, was the longest three-set match of the Open Era at 4:26 hours. The third set alone lasted 2:43 hours.

- Federer holds the Open Era record for the most finals appearances at one tournament: 15 in Basel, the ten finals in a row in Basel (2006-2015) are also a record.

- Federer is the only person in tennis history to win seven tournaments at least six times: Halle (10×), Basel (10×), Wimbledon (8×), Dubai (8×), Cincinnati (7×), Australian Open (6×), ATP Finals (6×).

- He is the only player to have won two tournaments on two different surfaces ten times each, namely the Gerry Weber Open in Halle on grass (2003-2006, 2008, 2013-2015, 2017, 2019) and the Swiss Indoors in Basel on hard court (2006-2008, 2010, 2011, 2014, 2015, 2017-2019).

- With 24 tournament wins, he is the most successful player at ATP Tour 500 tournaments.

- In the course of his professional career, he played 1750 matches in singles and doubles, in none of which he retired early.

Other books by United Library

https://campsite.bio/unitedlibrary

Milton Keynes UK
Ingram Content Group UK Ltd.
UKHW030807300124
436964UK00003B/5